# Robust  Watermarking Techniques

---

# Introduction

---

Digital image watermarking has gained a huge interest in the last decade among re- searchers. Having such a great group of people which provide a continuously growing list of proposed algorithms, it is rapidly finding solutions to its problems. However, still we are far away from being successful. Therefore, more and more people are entering the field to make the watermarking idea useful and reliable for digital world. Of these different watermarking algorithms, some smash others in terms of basic watermarking requirements like robustness, invisibility, processing cost, etc.

In this thesis, we study the how to protect ownership of digital image using the robust and blind watermarking technique. we evaluate the performance of the algorithm from the watermarking literature against again a selected set of attacks and distortions and try to figure out the properties of the methods that make them vulnerable or invulnerable against these attacks.

# Contents

# List of Figures

# Chapter   *1*

# Introduction

Recent years have seen a quick growth in the availability of digital multimedia content. Today, digital media documents can be distributed via the World Wide Web to a tremendous number of people without much attempt and money. Additionally, unlike traditional analog copying, with which the quality of the duplicated content is degraded, digital tools can easily produce large amount of perfect copies of digital documents in a short period. This ease of digital multimedia distribution over the Internet, together with the possibility of unlimited duplication of this data, threatens the intellectual property (IP) rights more than ever. Thus, content owners are eagerly seeking technologies that promise to protect their rights.

Cryptography is probably the most common method for protecting digital content since it has a well-established theoretical basis and developed very successfully as a science. The content is encrypted before delivery and a key is provided to the legitimate owner However, the seller is unable to discover how the product is handled after it is decrypted by the buyer.

Encryption protects the content during the transmission only. When transmitted to the receiver, data must be decrypted in order to be valuable. Once decrypted, the data is no longer protected and it becomes vulnerable. The buyer may turn out to be a pirate distributing illegal copies of the decrypted (unprotected) content. Therefore, encryption must be complemented with a technology that can continue to protect the valuabledata even after it is decrypted. This is the point where watermarking comes in. Digital watermarking technology is receiving increasing attention since it presents a possible solution for prohibiting copyright infringement of the multimedia data in open, highly uncontrolled environments where cryptography cannot be applied successfully.

## 1.1    Digital Watermarking

A digital watermark is a distinguishing piece of information that is adhered to the data (generally called cover or host data) that it is intended to protect. Watermarking embeds (generally hides) a signal directly into the data and the signal becomes an integral part of the data, travelling with the data to its destination. This way, the valuable data is protected as long as the watermark is present (and detectable) in it. At any given moment, the hidden signal can be extracted to get the copyright-related information. Thus, the goal of a watermark must be to always remain present in the host data. However, in practice the requirement is somewhat weaker than that: Depending on the application, a watermark is required to survive all the possible manipulations the host data may undergo as long as they do not degrade too much the quality of the document.

Digital watermarking is the process of embedding information into a digital signal which may be used to verify its authenticity or the identity of its owners, in the same manner as paper bearing a watermark for visible identification. In digital watermarking, the signal may be audio, pictures, or video. If the signal is copied, then the information also is carried in the copy. A signal may carry several different watermarks at the same time.

### 1.1.1    Visible Digital Watermarking

In visible digital watermarking, the information is visible in the picture or video. Typically, the information is text or a logo, which identifies the owner of the media. The image on the right has a visible watermark. When a television broadcaster adds its logo to the corner of transmitted video, this also is a visible watermark.

### 1.1.2   Invisible Digital Watermarking

In invisible digital watermarking, information is added as digital data to audio, picture, or video, but it cannot be perceived as such (although it may be possible to detect that some amount of information is hidden in the signal). The watermark may be intended for widespread use and thus, is made easy to retrieve or, it may be a form of Steganography, where a party communicates a secret message embedded in the digital signal. In either case, as in visible watermarking, the objective is to attach ownership or other descriptive information to the signal in a way that is difficult to remove. It also is possible to use hidden embedded information as a means of covert communication between individuals. One application of watermarking is in copyright protection systems,  which are in- tended to prevent or deter unauthorized copying of digital media. In this use, a copy deviceretrieves the watermark from the signal before making a copy; the device makes a decision whether to copy or not, depending on the contents of the watermark. Another application is in source tracing. A watermark is embedded into a digital signal at each point of distribution.If a copy of the work is found later, then the watermark may be retrieved from the copy andthe source of the distribution is known. This technique reportedly has
been used to detect the source of illegally copied movies.

**Digital watermarking techniques**

# 1.2   Robustness

A digital watermark is called fragile if it fails to be detectable after the slightest modi- fication. Fragile watermarks are commonly used for tamper detection (integrity proof). Modifications to an original work that clearly are noticeable, commonly are not referred to as watermarks.

A digital watermark is called semi-fragile if it resists benign transformations, but fails detection after malignant transformations. Semi-fragile watermarks commonly are used to detect malignant transformations.

A digital watermark is called robust if it resists a designated class of transformations. Robust watermarks may be used in copy protection applications to carry copy and no access control information.

# 1.3   Perceptibility

A digital watermark is called imperceptible if the original cover signal and the marked signal are (close to) perceptually indistinguishable.

A digital watermark is called perceptible if its presence in the marked signal is noticeable, but non-intrusive.

# 1.4   Capacity

The length of the embedded message determines two different main classes of digital watermarking schemes:

## 1.4.1   1-bit Watermark

The message is conceptually zero-bit long and the system is designed in order to detect the presence or the absence of the watermark in the marked object. This kind of watermarking scheme is usually referred to as zero-bit or presence watermarking schemes. Sometimes, this type of watermarking scheme is called 1-bit watermark, because a 1 denotes the presence (and a 0 the absence) of a watermark.

## 1.4.2   Multiple-bit Watermark

The message is a n-bit-long stream ( with $n =| m |$ ) or $M = \{0, 1\}^n$ and is modu- lated in the watermark. These kinds of schemes usually are referred to as multiple-bit watermarking or non-zero-bit watermarking schemes.

## 1.5    Embedding Method

A digital watermarking method is referred to as spread-spectrum if the marked signal is obtained by an additive modification. Spread-spectrum watermarks are known to be modestly robust, but also to have a low information capacity due to host interference.

A digital watermarking method is said to be of quantization type if the marked signal is obtained by quantization. Quantization watermarks suffer from low robustness, but have a high information capacity due to rejection of host interference.

A digital watermarking method is referred to as amplitude modulation if the marked signal is embedded by additive modification which is similar to spread spectrum method, but is particularly embedded in the spatial domain.

## 1.6    Difference between Watermarking and Encryption

The main difference between watermarking and encryption is that encryption disguises the data and protects it by making it unreadable without the correct decryption key, while watermarking aims to provide protection in its original viewable/audible form. Water-marking, like cryptography, needs secret keys to identify legal owners. The key is used to embed the watermark, and at the same time to extract or detect it. Only with a correct key can the embedded signal be revealed. While a single bit of information indicating that a given document is watermarked or not is sufficient sometimes, most applications demand extra information to be hidden in the original data. This information may consist of ownership identifiers, transaction dates, logos, serial numbers, etc., that play a key role when illegal providers are being tracked.

Watermarking can be used mainly for owner identification (copyright protection), to identify the content owner; fingerprinting, to identify the buyer of the content; for broad- cast monitoring to determine royalty payments; and authentication,to determine whether the data has been altered in any manner from its original form.

# Chapter *2*

# Related Work

For copy write protection of digital images our work has moved by a number of earlier works available in the literature that make use of digital image watermarking. A few of the considerable researches are briefly illustrated as follows: An asymmetrical water- marking method for copy write protection that satisfies the zero knowledge principle with the objective to defeat the weakness of contemporary symmetric watermarking methods is offered by jengnan Tzeng et al. [1].

Shang-Lin Hsieh et al.[2] presented a watermarking scheme for copywrite protection of color images. By the scheme the requirement of imperceptibily and robustness for a sensible watermarking scheme By the experiment it has been demonstrated that the resistanceof their scheme in opposition to many attacks for example cropping scaling, and JPEG compression.

In 2002, Joo et al. proposed a robust watermark scheme[19] by embedding a wa- termark into wavelet low-frequency sub-band [20]. It is briefly introduced as follows. First, an image with size of 512 by 512 pixels is transformed into wavelet coefficients by three-level wavelet transform (as shown in Fig. 1)

and extract the sub-band LL3 The extracted sub-band LL3 is further decomposed

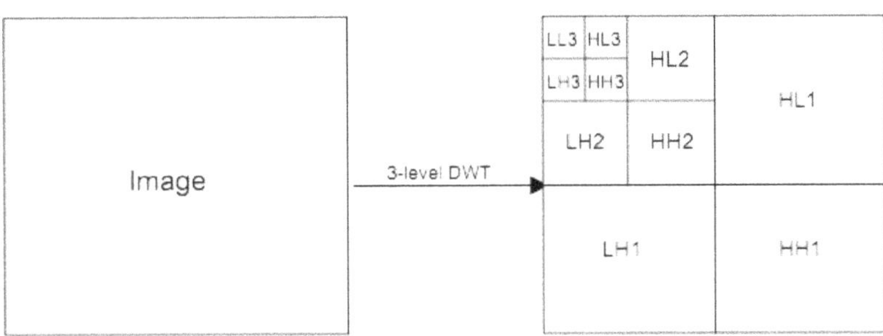


Figure 1: Three level wavelet decomposition of an image [22]

into four sub-bands and then three high- frequency sub-bands (LH4,HL4,andHH4) are set to zero. After performing inverse wavelet transform, its reference sub-band LL3 V is obtained. The information idx of embedding location in the watermark embedding process is obtained by sorting $| LL3 - LL3^r |$. Finally, the watermark information is embedded into the sub- band LL3 by $LL3 = LL3^r \pm k \times w(idx(i))$, where k is a factor for controlling embedding intensity and w is a pseudo-random binary sequence with the length of 1000 bits generated by using a seed, w belongs to{1, -1}. Besides, due to the fact that change to LL3 values also cause some change to its reference LL3 values, hence, the embedding process is repeated (the repeated times of embedding process are 10 times. in their paper). As the embedding process is repeated, the image quality is decreased but its reliability is increased.

In watermarking extraction process, the original image is required for obtaining the watermark embed- ding location. According to the embedding location, the watermark can be extracted by comparing the two sub-bands $LL3$ and $LL3^r$. Finally, the extracted water-mark is compared with the original watermark by similarity measure formula [20].

We know that, for an image, most of energy is concentrated on low-frequency and human eyes are sensitive to the change of low-frequency. Although the above scheme provides the characteristics of robustness and imperceptibility, but the embedding pro- cess is quite time-consuming. Besides, the original image is required in the watermark extractionprocess,which is impractical in real application.

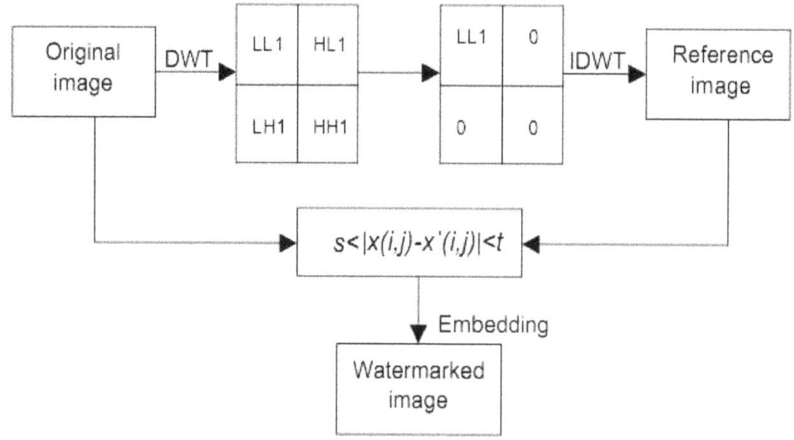


Figure 2: Watermark Embedding process [22]

## 2.1   Copyright Protection System

It is the time now to build the full copyright protection system. The now chart of the proposed copyright protection system is illustrated in figures 2 and 3. As appears in the figures 3 and 4, the proposed copyright protection system consists of: The Marking System, the Mark Detector System, and The Authors' Identification database.

The marking system is the embedder itself. It takes as input parameters: the image to be watermarked and the identification mark of the author (may be an image, a fingerprint of the author ... etc). The Mark detector is the extractor side of the algorithm. It takes as a parameter; the copyrighted image. It extracts the mark from it, and compares it to  a databaseof marks. According to a similarity measure between the extracted mark and a selected mark from the database, the system decides the author of the image. The au- thors' identification database is a database of some property of authors. The identification may be an image of the author, a fingerprint, or an identification number that uniquely identifies each author. The proposed system uses a grayscale image of the author as an identification mark. picture of the author embedded. Figure 4 shows the image of the author after extraction compared to the original in figure 3.

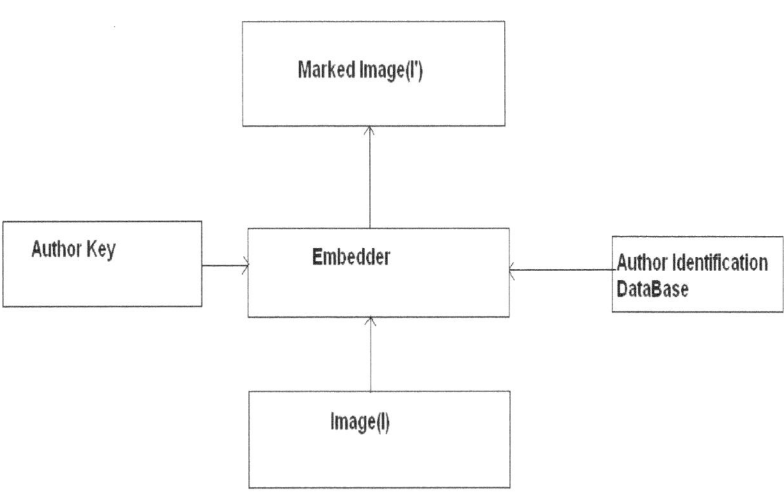


Figure 3: Work flow of marking system [21]

## 2.2   Private and Public Watermark Scheme

In recent years, watermarking has become an attractive topic and many watermarking schemes have been proposed [3-7]. Among these schemes, the ones which require the original information and secret keys for the watermarking extraction are called private watermark schemes. Schemes which require the watermark information and secret keys are called semi-private or semi-blind schemes. Schemes which need secret keys rather than the original information are called public or blind watermark schemes [8]. In general, the robustness of private watermark schemes is good to endure signal processing attacks.

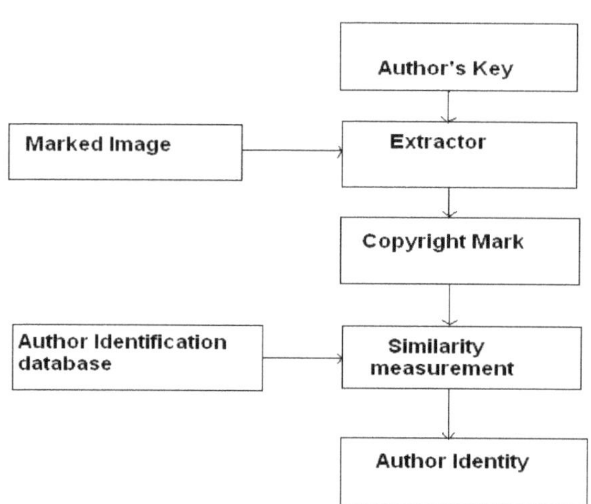


Figure 4: Work flow of mark detector system [21]

Chapter 3

# APPLICATIONS AND PROPERTIES

## 3.1  Applications

In this section, watermarking applications and their requirements are examined. The ma- jor applications of watermarking are owner identification/proof of ownership [6-8], authentication (also referred as content verification, data integrity or tamper proofing) [7, 8], transactional watermarks, copy control, covert communication, and broadcast moni- toring .

### 3.1.1  Owner Identification and Proof of Ownership

A traditional copyright notice in the form of date, owner added on an image or a video frame is no longer a safe way of guaranteeing copyrights . Although such annotations are still recommended, they can easily be cropped out or processed hence, removing or altering the ownership information. Hence, copyright violation harms the interests of the providers rather than those of customers. Since a digital watermark, once embedded, becomes an imperceptible and inseparable part of the host data, it can be used to provide copyright marking functionality. The intellectual property owner adds his/her copyright

information in the form of a high fidelity, robust, and secure watermark.

The level of security required to prove ownership is higher than that required for owner identification. Proving ownership means proving that a document owns to someone and that it does not belong to anyone else. This comes from the fact that a pirate can undermine the original watermark without removing it.

## 3.1.2    Transaction Tracking (Fingerprinting)

Transactional watermarks, also called fingerprints, allow an IP (intellectual property) owner or content distributor to identify the source of an illegal copy by marking each legal copy of the document with a separate, unique watermark. If a document marked with a transaction watermark is misused (distributed illegally), the owner can find out who is responsible. There are two well-known real-world applications for fingerprinting. One is the distribution of movie dailies. A movie daily is the result of each days photog- raphy and they are distributed to a number of people involved. Although these dailies are highly confidential, occasionally a daily is leaked to the press. The watermark, being dif- ferent in each copy, serves as a tracker to find the source of leakage. The other application was deployed by the now-defunct company DivX. Actually, they designed and marketed a new player, which placed a unique watermark to each video it played. If someone makes copies of this film after it is viewed then the watermark would appear on all the copies identifying the player on which it was played. If those copies are sold on a black market, then the DivX could obtain one of the copies and find the adversary or at least the player of the adversary.

## 3.1.3    Content Authentication

With the advance of computer tools available for digital signal processing, modifying a digital document is becoming easier while detecting that the content is modified becomes harder. Message authentication problem has been well studied in cryptography [10]. The solution offered by cryptography is a digital signature, and it is a widely accepted method. Only the authorized source knows the valid key for encryption, an adversary who tries to

change the message cannot create a corresponding valid signature for the modified mes- sage. The disadvantage of digital signatures is that they must be padded as metadata to the original data as separate information before transmission. It is thus easy to lose the signatures during daily usage, even without any bad-mannered operations. Format con- version is the best example to those situations. If the signature is saved to the header fields of some data format (e.g. JPEG), then it will be discarded when we switch to some other format with no space for a signature in the header. When the signature is lost, the work can no longer be authenticated. The superiority of watermarking comes at this point. Since the watermark information is carried directly on the bits of the original work, we do not lose them if the header field of the digital file is removed. Some authentication marks are designed to become invalid at the slightest modification on protected data. Those marks are called fragile watermarks. In signature embedding systems, signature calculation is host signal dependant since a signature is a summary of the data to be protected. How- ever, when we embed the signature in the data, the data content is modified. Even this modification is small; the signature might no more represent the modified data. To over- come this problem it is suggested to separate the data into two parts: one for signature calculation, and one for signature embedding .

### 3.1.4 Broadcast Monitoring

Commercials are vital for the survival of radio and TV channels. Companies book a specified time of the air on a specified time of the day and introduce their products to the audience and they pay for the time they book. The price they pay also varies from time to time in a day. Booking noon hours is much cheaper than booking the evening hours, which they call prime time. Therefore, companies carefully plan and prepare their commercials and put great importance on them. Thats why the companies have been using a broadcast monitoring system dating back at least 1975 [11]. It is not the commercials only that need to be monitored. Some news items may have hundreds of thousands of dollars value per hour. This makes them very vulnerable to intellectual property rights violations. Another usage of broadcast identification data is in competitive market research [12]. A company may want to know how much the competing company is investing on its new brand in the market and adjust its own marketing policy according to this data. A third possible

application is the detection of illegal (unauthorized) rebroadcasts of copyrighted material by pirate stations. Intellectual property owners will be more interested in these  types of systems [36]. One of the available products offering watermarking based broadcast monitoring and verification solutions is Verances ConfirMedia [13].

### 3.1.5   Copy Control

The applications that we mentioned so far have the philosophy of proving that a copyright infringement has occurred instead of trying to prevent the infringement to occur. The watermarks we mentioned are utilized after we suspect some content is modified or distributed illegally. However, with the help of an intelligent hardware we can have control over the duplication, modification, and distribution processes, which are the main sources of illegal action. Copy control technologies may serve as a deterrent against such actions. Encryption is once again a solution to the problem. The content is distributed to legitimate users in an encrypted format and only these users have a unique key for decryption. The key is in a special format that is difficult to duplicate and distribute. For example, satellite TV broadcast companies gives its customers a smart card (very much like the SIM cards of cellular phones), which is inserted into the decoder box, serving as the key. Without the key, the decoder cannot decrypt the incoming signals and all you can see is scrambled video.

### 3.1.6   Device Control

Device control is a broad category of applications in which specially designed devices react to the watermarks they detect in content. In 1953, Tomberlein et al. [14] described a system to distribute music to offices, stores and other premises. Broadcast is watermarked to mark the beginning and end of commercials, talk and other stuff other than music so that they are ignored and not aired in the office, store, etc.

## 3.2   Properties

Watermarks are generally desired to satisfy some requirements [17], [18] like robustness, tamper resistance (security), high capacity, fidelity, low computational cost, low falsepositive rate, etc. However, it is probably impossible to design a watermark that excels at allof these. The properties a watermarking scheme also depend greatly on the application at hand. Therefore, the properties a watermark should have are decided according to the application for which the watermark is designed. It is not necessary to have the best tamper resistance properties in a watermark that will be used, for example, to annotate the pictures you have in your home computer. For such an application, you may desire to have a watermark that betters in imperceptibility (fidelity) and capacity. Thus, it would be unfair to evaluate the properties of two such watermarking schemes according to the same standards. In this section, we will examine those properties in detail.

### 3.2.1  Robustness

We are living in a hacking world where it is very common that movies (actually all types of multimedia), software, documents, etc are duplicated and distributed without paying anything to their intellectual owners. This growing amount of illegal copying and distri- bution is the motivation that emerged the field of robust watermarking.

Robustness is an important issue for the watermarks that are not specially designed to be fragile. In general terms, a robust watermark is the one that resists (remains detectable after) common signal processing operations.

In general there should be no way in which the watermark can be removed or altered without sufficient degradation of the perceptual quality of the host data so as of render it unusable.

The properties stated above look very demanding. Only some extreme applications, in which the signal processing between the embedding and detection is unpredictable, require robustness against every possible distortion that does not destroy the value of the cover data.

Fortunately, in general, a watermark is not required to be robust against all possible manipulations. The robustness requirement is always finalized according to the applica- tion.

For some applications like broadcast monitoring or covert communication, a water- mark is supposed to survive lossy compression and transmission channel effects (low-pass filtering and additive noise), that is, the processing until the receiving party detects the watermark. It does not need to survive rotation, scaling, cropping, high-pass filtering, or other types of distortions that are not likely to occur during broadcast or travelling through a communication channel. After the watermark is detected successfully at the destination, either the watermarked data is erased or it becomes worthless, so protection is no more needed for that data.

In authentication applications, robustness is completely undesirable. Instead, a fragile watermark is required. We use fragile watermarks to understand if the data has been altered since it was watermarked.

### 3.2.2   Watermark Payload

Capacity of a watermarking system is the maximum amount of data (generally stated in bits) that can be inserted in the cover data. When we talk about the capacity, we implic- itly impose the fidelity requirement. Because embedding bits into a host signal requires modifying some of the host characteristics and the watermarked signal deviates from its original. In order to embed large amount of data into a multimedia signal without too much affecting the fidelity, properties of the human visual system (HVS) are utilized. Properties of the human visual system give us clues about the components (either in pixel domain or in a transform domain) that do not have a large effect on perceptual quality of the document. Then we can design the watermark such that it modifies those unper- cepted components in large amounts and other perceptually significant components are less affected.

### 3.2.3   Fidelity

A high fidelity watermark is a well-hidden signal such that it does not cause a perceptible degradation in the host (cover) data. Fidelity and quality are different terms and must not be confused. Fidelity is a measure of the similarity between signals before and after processing. Quality, on the other hand, is an absolute measure of appeal. It is possible to have high quality together with low fidelity and vice versa. You can watermark a greyscale, highly compressed, low resolution (hence low quality) video and it may well be impossible to distinguish this watermarked version form the original (hence high fidelity). If a watermark is not specially designed to be visible then it should not degrade the perceivedquality of the work. That is, the perceptual similarity between the original and watermarkedversions of the document must be as high as possible. This immediately implies the need for a good quality metric. It has been shown [17,18] that measures based on perceptual models yields more satisfactory results than the pixel-based models. The capacity and fidelity requirements are also application dependant.

### 3.2.4   Security

The security of watermarking techniques can be interpreted the same way as the security of encryption systems. For a watermarking technique to be truly secure, an unauthorised party should not be able to detect or remove an embedded watermark . the algorithms for embedding and extracting the watermark are exactly known since they are publicly available.

This requirement can be fulfilled in cryptography by the use of a secret key. Keys can be thought of some information (possibly random) that determine how messages are encrypted. A message encrypted by a given key can only be decrypted with the same key. Many watermarking systems are designed to use secret keys in an analogous manner. In such systems, the method by which messages are embedded in watermarks depends on a key, and a matching key must be provided to the receiver side to detect those marks. How- ever, the security requirements for watermarks are still somewhat different from those for ciphers. Ciphers prevent unauthorized reading and writing of documents, in that form, they can prevent certain types of attacks, but they do not provide protection for water- mark removal. Removing the watermark or masking it so that it can no more be extracted is analogous to the problem of signal jamming in military communications.

# Chapter  *4*

---

# Proposed Watermarking Algorithm

---

## 4.1  Preliminaries

Watermarking is, in essence, a form of communication where the sending side wishes to communicate a message from the watermark embedder to the watermark receiver. There- fore, it was instant and inevitable to try to fit watermarking into the traditional model of a communications system given in Figure 5. The encoder and decoder keys are not a part of the traditional model. They are added when secure communication is required.

When looked at as a communication task , the watermarking process can be split into three main steps: watermark generation and embedding (information transmission), possible attacks (transmission through the channel), and watermark retrieval (information decoding at the receiver side). There are two ways (models) in which a watermarking system can be mapped into the communications system above. The two models differ in the way they use the cover (original) image, in which we insert the watermark.

The first model interprets the cover image, I, as noise. Whether this noise will be used as side information or not is a matter of choice. If it is used as a side information (shown as a dashed arrow in Figure 6), then the watermark becomes a function of the cover image

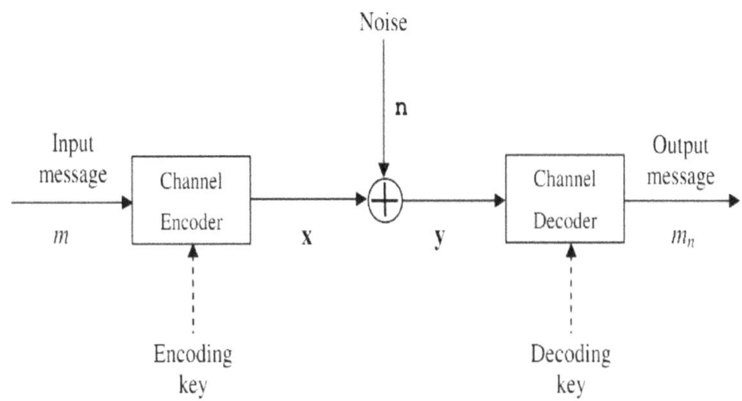


Figure 5: Standard model of a communication system [8]

and the key. A watermark embedder which accepts the original image as input is called an informed embedder, in contrast to a blind embedder which produces the watermark regardless of the original image content.

The second model regards the cover image not as a part of the transmission channel but as a second message to be transmitted along with the watermark in the same signal Iw. The model places two receivers for each component of the transmitted composite signal: a human being for the original image and a watermark detector for the water- mark. This model of watermarking is similar to the traditional communication systems like time-division or frequency-division multiplexing which transmit multiple messages over a single line. On the receiver side, the human receiver should perceive something close to the original cover image with ideally no interference from the watermark and the watermark detector should obtain the watermark message with no interference from the cover image. In the following discussion we will take the first model as our basis.

The duty of the embedder is first to map the massage m to a pattern (with the help of a watermark key, k) suitable for adding to the cover image and then to add the pattern, w, to the original image in a suitable way. As a result of this process, the watermarked image, Iw, which is going to be communicated, is produced. After the watermarked image is transmitted, it is processed in some way, which we model as an addition of noise, n. However, actual processes may be different than that. The watermarked image might

go under compression, decompression, digital-analog-digital conversions, audio or visual enhancements, and even malicious attacks which intend to remove the watermark.

At the receiving side, the watermark detector may be of one of the two configurations: blind (Figure 6) . If we are using an informed detector, the detection process consists of two steps. First, subtraction of the original image made available at the detector to obtain a noisy watermark pattern, wn. Then the pattern is decoded with the watermark key to extract the message as mn. Since the original image is subtracted from the received image, we can ignore the addition of the original image at a blind embedder, and the system looks very similar to the system in Figure 5.

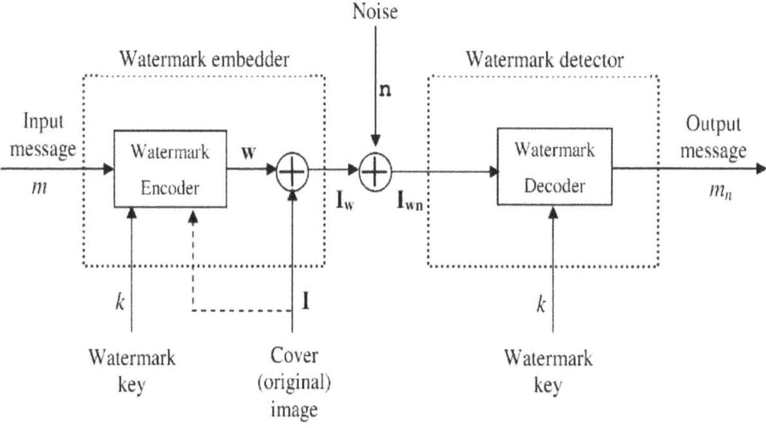


Figure 6: Watermarking system with a blind/informed embedder and a blind detector mapped into the communications model [8]

We can generalize the total watermark embedding process in the two steps first extracting a set of features (host features) from the host image, and then by modifying them according to the watermark content. The choice of the host features and the definition of the embedding rule have implications on watermark robustness and imperceptibility, which are the main concerns and challenges of the watermark embedding process.

## 4.2   Proposed Watermarking Algorithm

Proposed technique is totally based on DCT. Here block wise watermark embedding is done against the cropping attack. Before embedding the watermark for any host image we must calculate the gain factor. According to over approach gain factor will vary for two different host images . The proposed system here uses the DCT transform domain
.The embedding and extraction process are described in this section. The watermark embedding process is shown in fig 7.

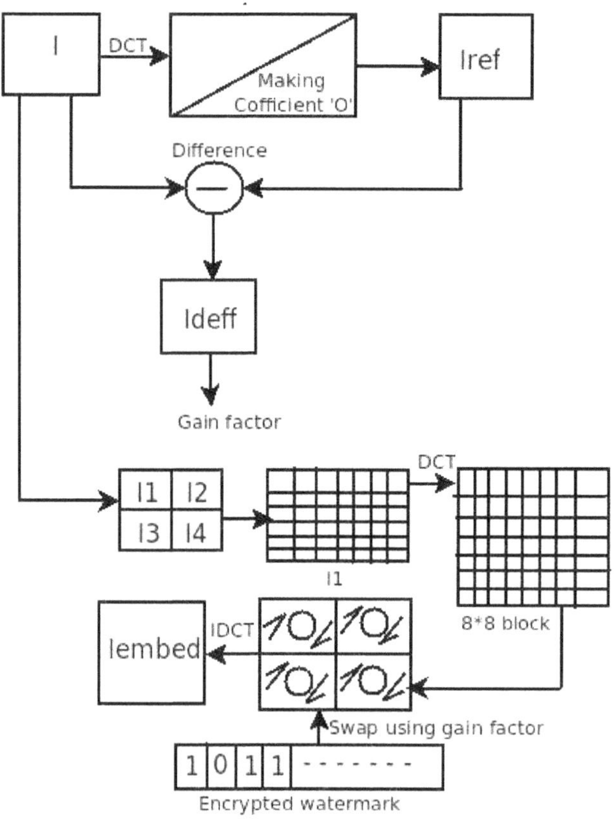


Figure 7: Diagram of watermark embedding process

# 4.3 Watermark embedding

The original image is a gray-level image with M by N pixels. The watermark W is a logo. They are defined as follows:

## 4.3.1 Gain factor calculation

In order to calculate the gain factor we need to follow these steps:

- First we will take the DCT of host imagethen convert DCT matrix in to upper trian- gular matrix.and after that we will take IDCT of upper triangular matrix of image. And finally we will get a reference image.

- we will calculate the difference between host image and reference image and the difference would be a matrix with some pixel values.from this matrix we will find the maximum and minimum values in it.so by using this difference we will calcu- late the gain factor.

$$Gainfactor = \frac{max(diff) - min(diff)}{2}$$

Gain factor will be used to find the changes in pixel values.

## 4.3.2   Watermark Encryption

- Generate a pseudo random matrix of the same size as the watermark size by using a secret key .i.e

$$S = s(i) : 0 \leq i \leq n, s(i) \in [0, 1]$$

- Encrypt the watermark by a bit-wise logical Exclusive-OR operation with S, i.e.

$$S(i) = i \oplus s(i)$$

Table 1: $8 \times 8$Block

| 1 | 2 | 3 | 4 | 5 | 6 | 7 | 8 |
|---|---|---|---|---|---|---|---|
| 9 | 10 | 11 | 12 | 13 | 14 | 15 | 16 |
| 17 | 18 | 19 | 20 | 21 | 22 | 23 | 24 |
| 25 | 26 | 27 | 28 | 29 | 30 | 31 | 32 |
| 33 | 34 | 35 | 36 | 37 | 38 | 39 | 40 |
| 41 | 42 | 43 | 44 | 45 | 46 | 47 | 48 |
| 49 | 50 | 51 | 52 | 53 | 54 | 55 | 56 |
| 57 | 58 | 59 | 60 | 61 | 62 | 63 | 64 |

## 4.3.3   Block division

In this section we will take the host image I and and perform the blocking operation means we divide the host image in to 4 blocks of size 256×256.And within each 256×256 block we will divide into 1024 blocks of size $8 \times 8$.

### 4.3.4 Watermark Embedding

In this section we will discuss the embedding process.How encrypted watermark image will embed in to the host image.

- We convert the encrypted watermark image in to vector. Then following operation will perform for each $8 \times 8$ blocks.

- Further divide $8 \times 8$ blocks in to 4 blocks.

- Skip the $1^{st}$ block as it is.

- Take the DCT of remaining three blocks

- If watermark bit is 1 then do following

    – Check if $m(value) > n(value) : m \in \{15, 43, 47\}, n \in \{22, 50, 54\}$

    – $M(value) = \frac{M(value)+gainfactor}{2}$

    – $N(value) = \frac{N(value)-gainfactor}{2}$


    _ Else swap the m(value) with n(value)then

    – $M(value) = \frac{M(value)+gainfactor}{2}$

    – $N(value) = \frac{N(value)-gainfactor}{2}$

- if watermark bit is 0 then do following

    – Check if $m(value) < n(value) : m \in \{15, 43, 47\}, n \in \{22, 50, 54\}$

- $M(value) = \dfrac{M(value)-gainfactor}{2}$

- $N(value) = \dfrac{N(value)+gainfactor}{2}$

  _ Else swap the m(value) with n(value)then

- $M(value) = \dfrac{M(value)-gainfactor}{2}$

- $N(value) = \dfrac{N(value)+gainfactor}{2}$

- Take IDCT of $8 \times 8$ block and We will repeat these above step for each $8 \times 8$ blocks, and finally we will get watermarked image

## 4.3.5   Watermark Extraction

The watermark extraction process does not require the original image.we utilize the sequence of embedding location to extract the watermark.

**Input: A Watermarked image Output:**
**Watermark $w^r$**

- Transform the watermarked image in to DCT coefficient

- Convert DCT coefficient matrix in upper triangular matrix and perform inverse discrete cosine transform(IDCT) and obtain its reference image.

- Divide watermarked image image in to 4 blocks of size $256 \times 256$.And within each $256 \times 256$ block we will divide into 1024 blocks of size $8 \times 8$

- Take the DCT of $8 \times 8$ within each $8 \times 8$ block do following

- Divide $8 \times 8$ blocks in to 4 blocks.

- Skip the $1^{st}$ block as it is.

- For remaining 3 blocks do

- We will take two variable $c_1$ and $c_2$ and check

- Check if $m(value) > n(value)$ then increment $c_1$ by 1 else

- increment $c_2$ by 1

- And check if $c1 > c2$ then watermark bit must be 1 else

- 0

- We get a vector v of size 1024 .convert that vector in to matrix
- Using the same secret key generate a $32 \times 32$ random matrix and convert it in to vector $v_s$
- Do bit wise Ex-OR operation of v and $v_s$
- Convert the result in to matrix, that would be matrix of watermark image

Figure 8: Original Image

Figure 9: Reference Image

Figure 10: Difference Image of the above two images

Figure 11: Watermark Image

Figure 12: Encrypted watermark

# Chapter 5

# The Experimental Results

In the following experiments, a gray-level image with size of 512 by 512 is used to as the original image and logo is used to as the watermark. After the watermark had been embedded into the original image, the PSNR (Peak Signal to Noise Ratio) of the water- marked image is 30.33 dB.

we choose the value of alpha to balance the tradeoff between the robustness and imperceptibility. Furthermore, the program development tool is MATLAB 7.0.

The proposed scheme transform the original image in to DCTcoefficient by then ,one lower sub bands are modified and obtain its reference image by performing inverse dis- crete cosine transform .After the watermark is embedded in to the original image, the PSNR(peak signal to noise ratio)is used to evaluate the quality of the watermarked im- age.the PSNR is defined as:

$$PSNR = 10\log_{10}\frac{255^2}{MSE}(dB),$$

$$MSE = \frac{1}{m \times n}\sum_{i=0}^{m-1}\sum_{j=0}^{n-1}(X_{ij} - X_{ij}^r)^2,$$

where $X_{ij}$ represents the original image and $X^r_{ij}$ represents the watermarked image.

In the following experiment,we use several image manipulations,including noise addition, ,filtering, and cropping ,on the watermarked images to evaluate the robustness of the proposed scheme.

## 5.1  Noise addition

We evaluate the robustness by adding Gaussian and salt pepper noise on the watermarked image.fig 13 , 14 and 15 show the Gaussian noise and fig 16 and 17 show the salt pep- per noise.the extracted watermark is still high similarity with the original watermark.It indicates that the proposed scheme is also robust to noise attack.

## 5.2   Filtering

We test the robustness by smoothing and sharpening the watermarked images.fig 18 and 19 show the resultant images by wiener filter and median filter with a window size of $2 \times 2$.

The test results show that the proposed method can also survive the filter attack.

## 5.3   Cropping

Fig. 20 show a cropped versions of the watermarked images in which 60% of the image has been removed This experimental result is well even though 60% of the watermarked image has been removed.

Watermarked Image

Recovered Message

Figure 13: The watermarked image by adding Gaussian noise with variance 0.01 (PSNR=28.81dB)

Table 2: Essential Information during Embedding ,Attack and Extraction

| Attack | Lena | baboon |
|---|---|---|
| **Gaussian  Noise**(*variance* = 0.01) | $PSNR = 28.81dB$ | $PSNR = 28.76$ |
| **Gaussian  Noise**(*variance* = 0.1) | $PSNR = 26.73dB$ | $PSNR = 26.71$ |
| **Gaussian  Noise**(*variance* = 0.5) | $PSNR = 24.67dB$ | $PSNR = 23.76$ |
| **Salt pepper Noise** (*variance* = 0.01) | $PSNR = 27.84dB$ | $PSNR = 27.76$ |
| **Salt pepper Noise**(*variance* = 0.1) | $PSNR = 24.84dB$ | $PSNR = 25.76$ |
| **Salt pepper Noise** (*variance* = 0.5) | $PSNR = 23.81dB$ | $PSNR = 22.76$ |
| **Weiner filter** $2 \times 2$ | $PSNR = 27.53dB$ | $PSNR = 28.76$ |
| **Median filter** $2 \times 2$ | $PSNR = 27.53dB$ | $PSNR = 28.76$ |

Figure 14: The watermarked image by adding Gaussian noise with variance 0.1 (PSNR=26.73dB)

Figure 15: The watermarked image by adding Gaussian noise with variance 0.5(PSNR=24.67dB)

Figure 16: The watermarked image by adding salt pepper noise with variance 0.01(PSNR=27.84dB)

Figure 17:  The watermarked image by adding salt pepper noise with variance 0.1(PSNR=24.84dB)

Figure 18: The blurred watermarked image (PSNR=27.53)

Figure 19: The blurred watermarked image (PSNR=25.59 )

Figure 20: Cropped version of watermarked images

# Chapter  6

# Conclusion

## 6.1  Conclusion

In this thesis ,we introduce joo et al.s scheme first ,which embeds a watermark in to low frequency of an image .however, for an image ,most of energy is concentrated on low frequency of an image ,and human eyes are sensitive to the change of low frequency.Although this scheme provides the characteristics of robustness and imperceptibility,but embedding process is quite time consuming.Besides,the original image is required in the watermark extraction process which is impractical in real application.

We utilize the concept of joo et al.s scheme and proposed a robust watermark scheme using encrypted watermark by transforming the original image in discrete cosine trans- form and embedding a encrypted watermark, the proposed scheme overcomes the weak robustness problem of embedding a watermark in the frequency domain. We can use a se- cure encryption algorithm,such as RSA, to increase security of the proposed scheme .the watermark extraction also does not require the original image so the application is more practical in real application  for ownership verification.the experimental results show that the proposed technique provides good image quality and robust to various attacks.


In summary ,the proposed method has the following contributions.firstly the water- mark extraction process does not require the original image.thus it may be applied eas- ily to internet.secondly,the proposed scheme overcomes the weak robustness problem of embedding a watermark in the frequency domain.thirdly,the embedded watermark can survive under various attacks.

ern, 'An Asymmetric SUB space
watermarking Method for copywrite protection In *IEEE Transactions on Signal processing* ,Vol .53,No.2 ,February 2005.

[2] Shang- Lin Heish,I-Ju Tsai,BIN-Yuan Huang and Jh jie jian . Protecting copyrights of
color images using a watermark scheme based on secret sharing and wavelet trans- form
In of multimedia,vol. 3, no. 4,October 2008

[3] T. Kalker, J-P. Linnartz, G. Depovere, and M. Maes On reliability of detecting elec-

tronic watermarks in digital images, In *in Proc. IX European Signal Processing Conf., vol 1, Island of Rhodes, Greece, Sept. 8-11, 1998, pp. 13-16.*

[4] *J. J. Quisquater, O. Bruyndonckx, and B. Macq Spatial method for copyright labeling of digital images, In* in Proc. 1995 IEEE Workshop Nonlinear Signal and Image Processing, North Marmaras, Greece, , *June 20-22, 1995, pp. 456- 459.*

[5] *Pitas and T. H. Kaskalis, Applying signatures on digital images In* in Proc. 1995 IEEE Workshop Nonlinear Signal and Image Processing, North Marmaras, Greece,, *June 20-22, 1995, pp. 460-463.*

[6] *E. Koch and J. Zhao. Toward robust and hidden image copyright labeling, In* Proc.


1995 IEEE Workshop Nonlinear Signal and Image Processing, North Marmaras, Greece, *June 20-22, 1995, pp. 452-455.*

[7] *W. Bender, D. Gruhl, and N. Morimoto, Techniques for data hiding In* Proc. SPIE, vol. 2420, , *pp. 40, 1995.*

[8] *S. Craver, N. Memnon, B. L. Yeo, and M. Yeung, , Resolving rightful ownerships with invisible watermarking techniques: Limitations, attacks and implications, In* IEEETrans. On Selected Areas of Communications, *16(4):573- 586, 1998.*

[9] *T. Ohsawa and M. Karita, Automatic telecasting or radio broadcasting monitoring system, In* United States Patent, *(3,760,275), 1973.*

[10] *D. R. Stinson, Cryptography: Theory and Practice, Boca Raton, In* FL: CRC Press, *1995.*

[11] *Rakesh Dugad, Krishna Ratakonda, and Narendra Ahuja, A new wavelet- based scheme for watermarking images, In* in Proceedings of the IEEE International Conference on Image Processing, ICIP, *'98, Chicago, IL, USA, October 1998.*

[12]*Jong Ryul Kim and Young Shik Moon, A robust wavelet-based digital watermark using level-adaptive thresholding, In* in Proceedings of the 6th IEEE International Conference

on Image Processing ICIP '99, page 202, Kobe, Japan, October 1999.

[13] G. Depovere, T. Kalker, and J. P. Linnartz, Improved watermark detection using filtering before correlation, Proc. 5th IEEE Int. Conf. Image Processing ICIP98, vol. I, Chicago, IL, Oct. 4-7 1998, pp. 430-434.

[14] J. Cox, Matt L. Miller, Electronic Watermarking: The First 50 Years, In Proceedings of the IEEE 2001 Int. Workshop on MultiMedia Signal Processing, 2001.),

[15] William M. Tomberlin, Louis G. MacKenzie, and Paul K. Bennett, System for transmitting and receiving coded entertainment programs, In United States Patent, 2,630,525, 1953.

[16] R. S. Broughton and W. C. Laumeister, Interactive videomethod and apparatus, States Patent, 4,807,031, 1989.

[17] R. G. Van Schyndel, A. Z. Tirkel, and C. F. Osborne, Towards a robust digital watermark, In in Dicta-95, pp. 504-508, Nanyang Technological University, Singapore, December 5-8, 1995.

[18] I. J. Cox and M. L. Miller, A review of watermarking and the importance of percep- tual modeling, In Proceedings of SPIE, Human Vision Electronic Imaging II, vol. 3016, pp.92-99, 1997.

[19] S. Joo, Y. Suh, J. Shin, H. Kikuchi, S.-J. Cho, , A new robustwatermark embedding into wavelet DC components In ETRI Journal 24 (5) (2002) 401404.

[20] .J. Cox, J. Kilian, F.T. Leighton, T. Shamoon, , Secure spread spectrum watermarking for multimedia In IEEE Transactions on Image Processing 6 (12) (1997) 1673 1687.

[21] Dr.M.A. Dorairangaswamy Protecting Digital-Image Copyrights: A Robust and Blind Watermarking Scheme In IEEE Vol.:9, No. 4, pp. 423-27, 2009.

[22] Jiang-Lung Liu, Der-Chyuan Lou *, Ming-Chang Chang, Hao-Kuan Tso A

*robust watermarking scheme using self-reference image*

*In* Elsevier Computer Standards  Interfaces 28 (2006) 356  367